Echoes of Eternity:

The Kalabhairava Ashtakam

G. VARUN YADAV

Qurate
qratebooks.com

Echoes of Eternity:

The Kalabhairava Ashtakam

G Varun Yadav

Published in 2025

© Published by

Qurate Books Pvt. Ltd.
Goa 403523, India
www.quratebooks.com
Tel: 1800-210-6527, Email: info@quratebooks.com

ISBN: 978-93-58988-01-7

Author's Note

With the deepest reverence and devotion, I humbly offer this book on the Kalabhairava Ashtakam to Lord Shiva, the eternal protector and fountainhead of divine wisdom. Every word of this work is a reflection of His guidance and blessings, without which this journey would not have been possible.

I wish to express my profound gratitude to The Sanskrit Channel on YouTube for its tireless efforts in bringing the beauty and depth of Sanskrit scriptures to life. Your dedication to preserving and sharing this timeless wisdom has been a beacon of inspiration on my spiritual journey.

This book is lovingly dedicated to my cherished companions—Kutti, Rani, Chintu, Boxy, Buggie, and Kallu. Each of them embodies the virtues of loyalty, guardianship, and unconditional love, reflecting the protective essence of Lord Kalabhairava. Dogs, often regarded as symbols of vigilance and strength, serve as a daily reminder of the divine presence in my life. To me, they are far more than pets; they are my guardian angels, silently watching over me with unwavering devotion and boundless affection.

May this work inspire readers to connect with the powerful energy of Lord Kalabhairava and to find solace, strength, and protection in His divine embrace.

With heartfelt gratitude,

G. Varun Yadav

Contents

1
INTRODUCTION

The Kalabhairava Ashtakam is a sacred hymn composed by the great philosopher and saint **Adi Shankaracharya,** honoring Lord Kalabhairava, a formidable and compassionate aspect of Lord Shiva.

Kalabhairava is revered as the Lord of Time (Kala) and the guardian of dharma. His presence is both awe-inspiring and comforting, as he embodies the power to destroy ignorance and evil while guiding devotees toward spiritual liberation. Through its eight poetic verses, the hymn vividly depicts Kalabhairava's divine qualities and cosmic role, making it a profound spiritual treasure for seekers.

Lord Kalabhairava's significance is deeply rooted in Hinduism. He is said to have manifested to restore balance and uphold dharma, representing the fierce and protective aspect of Shiva. His form, adorned with serpents, wielding divine weapons, and surrounded by an aura of mystery, reflects his role as a destroyer of negativity and protector of truth. At the same time, his compassionate nature shines through, offering solace, courage, and spiritual freedom to those who surrender to him.

The Kalabhairava Ashtakam is more than a hymn of praise—it is a spiritual guide that inspires introspection and transformation. Chanting or meditating on this hymn is believed to bring mental clarity, inner strength, and liberation from fear. As the master of time, Kalabhairava teaches us the impermanence of worldly life and the importance of aligning our lives with eternal truths. The hymn serves as a bridge between the material and the spiritual spheres, helping devotees transcend the fear of mortality and connect with the divine essence within themselves.

Kalabhairava is especially revered in Shaivism, where he is worshipped as a guardian deity who protects devotees and removes obstacles on their spiritual journey. His temples, particularly those in Varanasi and Ujjain, are considered powerful centers of devotion, attracting seekers who wish to experience his divine presence.

This book seeks to unravel the profound meaning and timeless wisdom of the Kalabhairava Ashtakam. Each verse reveals a unique facet of Lord Kalabhairava, blending poetic beauty with spiritual depth. By delving into its teachings, we can uncover practical and philosophical insights that illuminate our path and lead us toward liberation. Through this journey, the hymn reminds us that surrendering to Lord Kalabhairava is not just an act of devotion but a step toward understanding the eternal nature of existence.

2

KALABHAIRAVA

Figure 1: *Kalabhairava swaroopa*

Kalabhairava is a Fierce and powerful manifestation of Lord Shiva, revered as the guardian and ruler of time (Kala). In Hindu tradition, he is the protector of cosmic order, a destroyer of all illusions, symbolizing the inevitable passage of time that governs all creation. Kalabhairava is often depicted as a fearsome deity, dark in complexion, adorned with skulls and serpents, holding a trident and a drum, and accompanied by a dog, his sacred vehicle. His terrifying appearance signifies his role as the annihilator of ignorance and the remover of obstacles on the spiritual path.

The origins of Kalabhairava are deeply rooted in the Puranic lore. According to one legend, Kalabhairava emerged from Shiva's wrath when the creator god Brahma exhibited arrogance. To humble Brahma, Shiva assumed the form of Kalabhairava and severed Brahma's fifth head, symbolically curbing his pride. This act also reinforced the idea that no being, not even the creator, is beyond the bounds of time and cosmic law. As penance for this act, Kalabhairava wandered as a mendicant, carrying Brahma's skull (Kapala), a reminder of the inevitability of time and mortality.

Kalabhairava is also closely associated with the protection of sacred spaces and the dispelling of negative energies. As the guardian deity of Kashi (Varanasi), he is believed to oversee the karmic deeds of individuals and grant liberation (Moksha) to those who surrender to him. Pilgrims often pay homage to Kalabhairava in the belief that he helps transcend the cycles of birth and death. His worship involves offerings of black sesame seeds, oil lamps, and prayers to invoke his blessings for protection, prosperity, and spiritual progress.

Philosophically, Kalabhairava represents the ultimate reality that transcends time. While time governs the mortal world, Kalabhairava embodies the timeless truth of existence. His fierce form serves as a reminder of life's impermanence and the need to seek eternal truths beyond the transient material world. The name "Bhairava" itself signifies the one who instills awe and fear, urging devotees to confront their fears and embrace transformation.

Kalabhairava is also worshiped as the master of the eight directions (Ashta Bhairavas), with each direction symbolizing a facet of life and existence. Together, they represent the totality of creation under his protection. In the Tantric tradition, he is revered as a gateway to deeper spiritual realization and as a guide who leads seekers toward liberation by annihilating the ego and false identities.

In essence, Kalabhairava is not only the guardian of time and cosmic order but also a compassionate deity who aids devotees in overcoming their limitations and realizing their divine potential. His worship is both an acknowledgment of the inexorable power of time and a pathway to transcendence and liberation.

3

ASHTAKAM

An Ashtakam is a Form of devotional hymn in Sanskrit poetry, consisting of eight verses (hence the name, derived from "Ashta," meaning "eight" in Sanskrit). Each verse in an Ashtakam is crafted to glorify a deity, express devotion, or convey profound philosophical truths. Ashtakams are a significant part of Hindu religious and spiritual literature and are often recited during prayers, meditations, or spiritual practices.

Structure of an Ashtakam

The Ashtakam typically follows a rhythmic and metrical structure, designed to facilitate easy recitation and memorization. Each verse, or stanza, is usually composed of four lines (quatrains) and adheres to a specific meter (chandas). This structured rhythm not only adds to the hymn's poetic beauty but also makes it an effective tool for meditation, as the rhythmic chanting can help align the mind with the divine.

The eight verses often progress in a way that takes the devotee through a journey—starting with praise and adoration of the deity, moving through descriptions of their divine qualities, and concluding with a plea for blessings or liberation.

Purpose and Importance of an Ashtakam

- **Devotional Offering:**
  Ashtakams are a heartfelt way for devotees to express their love and devotion to a deity. They often include descriptions of the deity's form, attributes, and deeds, creating a vivid and intimate connection between the devotee and the divine.

- **Spiritual Growth:**
  Chanting or meditating on an Ashtakam is considered a powerful spiritual practice. The repetition of sacred sounds purifies the mind, focuses attention, and helps transcend worldly distractions.

- **Philosophical Insights:**
  Many Ashtakams are rich in philosophical content, offering insights into the nature of the divine, the self, and the universe. For example, the Nirvana Ashtakam by Adi Shankaracharya explores the essence of the soul and ultimate liberation (moksha).

- **Accessibility:**
  The eight-verse format makes Ashtakams concise yet profound, making them accessible to devotees who wish to engage in daily worship or contemplation.

Famous Ashtakams in Hindu Tradition

- **Kalabhairava Ashtakam:**
  Dedicated to Lord Kalabhairava, this hymn extols his role as the Lord of Time and a fierce protector of dharma.

- **Shiva Ashtakam:**
  A hymn devoted to Lord Shiva, emphasizing his attributes as the ultimate reality and destroyer of ignorance.

- **Govinda Ashtakam:**
  A prayer to Lord Krishna in his form as Govinda, celebrating his divine play and compassion.

- **Ganga Ashtakam:**
  A hymn in praise of the holy river Ganga, symbolizing purity and spiritual liberation.

The Role of Ashtakams in Daily Life

Ashtakams serve as tools for spiritual awakening and emotional solace. The simplicity of their structure and the depth of their content make them versatile for various contexts, whether sung in temples, recited during personal worship, or chanted during group prayers. Beyond their religious significance, the poetic beauty of Ashtakams appeals to those interested in Sanskrit literature and philosophy.In essence, an Ashtakam is not just a hymn—it is a bridge between the finite and the infinite, a means to connect the devotee's heart with the divine, and a vessel for transmitting timeless spiritual wisdom.

4

DECIPHERING THE KALABHAIRAVA ASHTAKAM

Rava Means Sound, while Bhairava means beyond sound. The entire world is made up of frequencies and vibrations. Bhairava is the one who transcends the physical vibrations or sounds. Kala refers to emptiness or darkness, and Kalabhairava is the form of Shiva that exists beyond emptiness and darkness. Kalabhairava remains before the formation and after the dissolution of the physical world, representing a state of existence that is eternal. Kalabhairava Ashtakam is a hymn sung in praise of Kalabhairava, celebrating histranscendental nature.

Structure of the Kalabhairava Ashtakam

Each line of the eight shlokas consists of 15 syllables.The hymn is composed in a poetic meter called tūṇaka chandas, which means "to expand" or "to fill."The pattern of syllables in tūṇaka is alternating, with one long syllable followed by one short syllable. The rhythm of each syllable follows this pattern:

naa na-naa na-naana-naana-naana-naana-naana-naa

This structure emphasizes the cosmic rhythm, mirroring the very essence of Kalabhairava—beyond sound, beyond emptiness, and beyond time itself.

4.1 Shloka 1

देवराजसेव्यमानपावनांघ्रपिङ्कजं

devarAjasevyamAnapAvanAMghripankajaM

व्यालयज्ञसूत्रमिन्दुशेखरंकृपाकरम्।

vyAlayajnasUtramindushekharaMkRpAkanam

नारदादियोगिवृन्दवन्दितंदिगंबर

nAradAdiyogivRndavanditaMdigambaraM

काशिकापुराधनिाथकालभैरवंभजे॥१॥

KashikApurAdhinAthakAlabhairavaM bhaje

Made easy to read:

Devaraja-Sevyamana-Pavana-Angri-Pankajam,

Vyala-Yagna-Suthram-Indu-Shekaram-Krupakaram,

Naradadhi-Yogi-Vrundha-Vandhitham-Digambaram,

Kashika-Pura-Adhinatha-Kalabhairavam-Bhaje.

The first word to understand here is 'Bhaje,' which means 'I worship.' This simple yet powerful declaration sets the tone for devotion and signifies surrender to the deity being praised. ***The phrase 'Kashika Pura Adhinatha' refers to Kalabhairava as the ruler of the holy city of Kashi. The full line 'Kashika Pura Adhinatha Kalabhairavam Bhaje' translates to "I worship Kalabhairava , the ruler of the city of Kashi."***

Since this key line is repeated at the end of each of the eight shlokas, we will not explain it again and again. Its presence in all the shlokas serves as a constant reminder of Kalabhairava's connection to Kashi and his role as the cosmic guardian of time and transformation.

The remaining three lines in the shloka describe various attributes of Kalabhairava. Each attribute can be identified by looking for word clusters ending in **'AM' or 'aM,'** which indicate the Dvitiya Vibhakti (objective case), where the object in a sentence is implied.

The word 'Digambaram' means one who has the directions (Dik) as his clothes (Ambara). This implies that Kalabhairava, as a personified form, roams naked, without attachment to the physical body. Metaphorically, 'Digambara' refers to the non-physical aspect of Kalabhairava, unclothed and unlimited, pervading the infinite expanse of the universe.

The next attribute, 'Vanditam,' means worshipped.

'Yogi-Vrnda' refers to 'a group of yogis,' and 'Narada-Adi' means 'Narada and others.''Kripakaram' means one who is compassionate, and 'Indu-Shekaram' means the one who has the moon over his head. The moon, referred to as 'Indu,' shares its origin with the word 'Bindu,' which means a drop of nectar or Amrita. Having the moon depicted on his head symbolizes the intoxicating bliss of a fully blossomed Sahasrara Chakra.The moon on his head is in its sixteenth state, an immortal, changeless state beyond the mortal phases of waxing and waning. Lord Kalabhairava bears it to signify his immortality and changeless nature.

'Vyala-Yajna-Sutram' refers to one who wears a serpent (Vyala) as the sacred thread of Yajna. The sacred thread represents austerity, penance, and Vedic conduct. The fierce serpent symbolizes that even something ferocious is transformed into a symbol of purity and austerity through his divine presence.

His attributes, such as the snake (symbolizing time) and the moon (symbolizing the mind), depict his control over time and consciousness.

'Deva Raja Sevya Mana Pavangri Pankajam' means 'the one whose pure lotus-like feet are worshipped by Indra, the king of Devas.' Even Indra, the ruler of heaven, worships Bhairava, signifying that anyone desiring heavenly pleasures can worship him for their fulfillment.'Angri' means feet, and 'Pankaja' means lotus.'Pavana' means pure, and 'Sevyamana' means serviced or worshipped.

Summary:

'I worship the main ruler of the city of Kashi, Kalabhairava, who is clothed in nothing but the directions themselves, who is worshipped by groups of yogis like Narada, who is compassionate, who wears a snake as his sacred thread of yajna, and whose pure lotus-like feet are worshipped by Indra, the king of the Devas.'

4.2. *Shloka 2*

भानुकोटभिास्वरंभवाब्धतिारकंपरं

bhAnukoTibhAsvaraMbhavAbdhitArakaMparaM

नीलकण्ठमीप्सतिार्थदायकंत्रलिोचनम्।

nIlakaNThamIpsitArthadAyakaMtrilocanam

कालकालमंबुजाक्षमक्षशूलमक्षरं

kAlakAlamaMbujAkshamakshashUlamaksharaM

काशकिापुराधनािथकालभैरवंभजे॥२॥

KashikApurAdhinAthakAlabhairavaM bhaje 2

Made easy to read :

Bhanu-Koti-Bhasvaram-Bhavabdhi-Tarakam-Param

Nila-Kantham-Iipsita-Artha-Dayakam-Trilocanam

Kala-Kalam-Ambujakasham-Akshashulam-Aksharam

Kashika-Pura-Adhinatha-Kalabhairavam-Bhaje.

'Ksharam' means 'to decay' or 'to perish,' while 'Aksharam' refers to something imperishable or eternal. This attribute signifies that Kalabhairava is imperishable and eternally youthful. The word 'Aksha' means bone, and 'Shula' refers to a trident. So, 'Aksha-Shulam' indicates that Kalabhairava carries a trident made of bone.

Another interpretation for Akṣhashulam - Lord is the embodiment of omkara and to him all the other syllables from 'a' to 'Ksha' are his weapons, his powers. The letters a (अ) to ksha (क्ष) represent the 50 letters of the alphabet in the Akshamalika Upanishad. Ambuja-Aksham means 'one with eyes like lotuses' (Ambuja means lotus, and aksha means eyes). Kala-Kalam has several interpretations. Kala can mean time, darkness, or even death, symbolizing the God of Death, Lord Yama. Therefore, Kala-Kala can be interpreted as 'the one who is darker than darkness,' 'the embodiment of eternal time,' or 'the one who caused the death of Yama.' This last interpretation is based on the story where Lord Shiva saves his devotee, Markandeya,from untimely death at the hands of Lord Yama. The attribute 'Tri-Lochanam' means one with three eyes(Lochana means eyes, and Tri denotes three). Shiva's third eye is represented physically on his forehead and spiritually symbolizes the fully activated Ajna chakra, representing pure perception and logic, free from worldly attachments. 'Iipsita-Artha-Dayakam' means the one who grants the objectives (artha) of our desires (Iipsita). 'Nila-Kantham' refers to Kalabhairava as having a blue throat, which refers to a story where Lord Shiva swallows the deadly poison from the churning of the ocean (Samudra Manthan). It also refers to the Vishuddhi chakra, associated with the color blue.

'Param' means 'the supreme' or the one who is of beyond, and Bhava-Abdhi-Tarakam indicates that Kalabhairava is the one who helps us cross the ocean (abdhi) of existence (bhava), freeing us from the cycle of rebirth. 'Bhanu-Koti-Khasvaram' portrays Kalabhairava as shining with the radiance (Bhasvaram) of countless suns (Koti means series, and Bhanu means sun).

Summary:
'I worship Lord Kalabhairava, the supreme ruler of the city of Kashi, who shines with the radiance of countless suns, helps us cross the ocean of existence, is beyond all, has a blue neck, grants the objects of our desires, has three eyes, can end death itself, has lotus-like eyes, wields a trident made of bone, and is eternal and imperishable.'

4.3. Shloka 3

शूलटंकपाशदण्डपाणिमादिकारणं

shUlaTaMkapAshadaNDapANimAdikAraNaM

श्यामकायमादिदेवमक्षरंनिरामयम्।

shyAmakAyamAdidevamakSharaMnirAmayam

भीमविक्रमंप्रभुंविचित्रताण्डवप्रियं

bhImavikramaMprabhuMvichitratANDavapriyaM

काशिकापुराधिनाथकालभैरवंभजे॥३॥

KashikApurAdhinAthakAlabhairavaM bhaje 3

Made easy to read:

Shula-Tanka-Pasha-Danda-Panim-Aadi-Karanam

Shyama-Kayam-Aadi-Devam-Aksharam-Nir-Aamayam

Bhima-Vikramam-Prabhum-Vichitra-Tandava-Priyam

Kashika-Pura-Adhinatha-Kalabhairavam-Bhaje. 3

'Panim' means one who holds in his hands. What does he hold? He holds the Shula (trident), Tamka (Hand drum), Pasha (noose), and Danda (staff). Hence, 'Shuula-Tanka-Pasha-Danda-Panim' signifies his dominion over these divine instruments.

The trident symbolizes Lord Bhairava's mastery over three core powers: Icchā shakti (desire and thought), Kriyā shakti (action), and gyāna shakti (wisdom). Its prongs represent the three gunas (satva, rajas, tamas), the three states of consciousness (wakefulness, dream, deep sleep), three sacred fires, and the three tenses of time (past, present, future). These forces serve as his weapons. The axe represents truth and wisdom, cutting through ignorance and falsehood, while his staff embodies his authority to enforce justice, purify beings, and govern time and death. Bhairava transcends even death, embodying the ultimate divinity as described in the Upanishads.

The following attribute is 'Adi-Karanam,' meaning the origin or cause of all beginnings. The word 'Shyama-Kayam' indicates that his body (kaya) is of a dark complexion (shyama), symbolizing the vast darkness of existence that Kalabhairava represents. The attribute 'Adi-Devam' signifies that he is the first among the devas or celestial beings. As we saw in the second shloka, 'Aksharam' depicts Kalabhairava as a yogi who remains eternally youthful. The word 'Ama' in Sanskrit means sickness or disease. Kalabhairava is described as 'Niramayam,' indicating he is free from afflictions and, as an aspect of creation, devoid of any deterioration. This also signifies that he is immune to illness, as his form is not composed of the three gunas (satva, rajas, tamas), but rather of shuddhasatva (pure satva). His body is not made of flesh and bone; instead, he embodies sat (existence), chit (consciousness), and ānanda (bliss).

'Bhima-Vikramam' refers to one who possesses enormous (Bhima) valor (vikramam). Kalabhairava is further described with the word 'Prabhum,' meaning he is the supreme lord of creation. The final attribute, 'Vichitra-Tandava-Priyam,' reveals that Kalabhairava is fond (priyam) of the cosmic dance (tandavam), which is wonderfully (vichitra) diverse. His dance serves as a profound expression of the five great cosmic deeds: creation, protection, destruction, disappearance, and blessing. With each movement, he brings forth the creation of the universe, ensures its protection, ushers in its destruction for renewal, symbolizes its dissolution back into the divine, and bestows blessings upon all beings. Through his dance, he manifests and embodies the entire cyclical nature of existence.

Summary:

I worship the main ruler of the city of Kashi, Kalabhairava, who holds a spear, a hand drum, a noose, and a staff in his four hands; who is the cause of all beginnings, who is of a dark complexion, who is the first of the celestial beings, who is undecaying and eternal, who is free from all afflictions, who is of an enormous valor, who is the lord of creation, and who is fond of the fierce cosmic dance, called as tandava.'

4.4 Shloka 4

भुक्तिमुक्तिदायकंप्रशस्तचारुविग्रहं

bhuktimuktidAyakaMprashastachAruvigrahaM

भक्तवत्सलंस्थितिंसमस्तलोकविग्रहम्।

bhaktavatsalaMsthitaMsamastalokavigraham

नकि्वणन्मनोज्ञहेमकङि्कणीलसत्कटिं

nikvaNanmanojnahemakinkiNIlasatkaTiM

काशिकापुराधिनाथकालभैरवंभजे॥४

KashikApurAdhinAthakAlabhairavaM bhaje 4

Made easy to read:

Bhukti-Mukti-Dayakam-Prashasta-Caru-Vigraham

Bhakta-Vatsalam-Sthitam-Samasta-Loka-Vigraham

Nikvanan-Manojnya-Hema-Kinkini-Lasat-Katim

Kashika-Pura-Adhinatha-Kalabhairavam-Bhaje. 4

In the phrase 'Bhukti-Mukti-Dayakam,'Bhukti refers to nourishment, and Mukti signifies liberation from bondage. Kalabhairava is the one who grants (dayakam) both nourishment and liberation (Bhukti-Mukti-Daayakam).

The next attribute, 'Prashasta-Charu-Vigraham,' describes Kalabhairava's form (vigraha) as both glorious (prashasta, meaning reputation or glory) and beautiful (charu).'Vatsa,' means a child, and 'Vatsalya' denotes the love one feels for a child. Thus, 'Bhakta-Vatsalam' portrays Kalabhairava as one who lovingly holds his devotees (bhaktas) as if they were his own children.

The attribute 'Stitham,' means 'firmly established,' and 'Samastha-Loka-Vigraham' depicts Kalabhairava as the embodiment of all the worlds.

A significant compound word in the shloka, 'Nikvanan-Manojnya-Hema-Kinkini-Lasat-Katim,' translates as the one who has a jingling, beautiful (lasat) golden bell (hema-kinkini) around his waist (katim) that charms the mind (manojna), heralding his arrival with its jingling sound (nikvanan).

Summary:

'I worship the supreme ruler of the city of Kashi, Kalabhairava, who grants both sustenance and liberation, who has a beautiful and glorious form, who lovingly embraces his devotees as his own children, who is firmly established, who embodies all the worlds, and who wears a golden bell around his waist, jingling melodiously and charming the mind, announcing his divine presence!'

4.5 Shloka 5

धर्मसेतुपालकंत्वधर्ममार्गनाशकं

dharmasetupAlakaMtvadharmamArganAshakaM

कर्मपाशमोचकंसुशर्मदायकंविभुम्।

karmapAshamochakaMsusharmadAyakaMvibhum

स्वर्णवर्णकेशपाशशोभितांगनिर्मलं

svarNavarNakeshapAshashobhitAMganirmalaM

काशिकापुराधिनाथकालभैरवंभजे॥५॥

KashikApurAdhinAthakAlabhairavaM bhaje 5

Made easy to read:

Version 1:

Dharma-Setu-Palakam-Tva-Adharma-Marga-Nashakam

Karma-Pasha-Mochakam-Su-Sharma-Dayakam-Vibhum

Svarna-Varna-Khesha-Pasha-Shobhitanga-Nirmalam

Kashika-Pura-Adhinatha-Kalabhairavam-Bhaje. 5

Version 2:

Dharma-Setu-Palakam-Tva-Adharma-Marga-Nashakam

Karma-Pasha-Mochakam-Su-Sharma-Dayakam-Vibhum

Svarna-Varna-Khesha-Pasha-Shobhitanga-Mandalam

Kashika-Pura-Adhinatha-Kalabhairavam-Bhaje. 5

'Kalabhairava is described with several profound attributes that highlight his divine essence. The first attribute, 'Dharma-Setu-Palakam,' signifies Kalabhairava as the protector and upholder of the path of dharma. Here, dharma is understood as the cosmic law of sustenance, derived from the root word 'dharana,' meaning to hold or sustain. Dharma is often described as a bridge that connects the jeevātmā (soul) to the paramātmā (Supreme Being).

The next attribute, 'Tva-Adharma-Marga-Nashakam,' describes Kalabhairava as the destroyer of the path of adharma (unrighteousness). He eradicates unrighteous actions and the very concept and allure of adharma, ensuring that no one is tempted or able to tread that path. Similarly, 'Karma-Pasha-Mochakam' portrays Kalabhairava as the liberator who frees us from the bondage of compulsive actions, known as karma. The attribute

'Su-Sharma-Dayakam' highlights his role as the bestower of supreme protection and well-being, while 'Vibhum' denotes his extraordinary and boundless existence.

Another significant attribute, 'Svarna-Varna-Khesha-Pasha-Shobhitanga-Nirmalam,' reveals Kalabhairava's fierce and radiant nature. The phrase describes his golden flaming locks of hair, which illuminate his pure and resplendent limbs. Adi Shankaracharya beautifully illustrates this radiance as a reflection of Kalabhairava's divine brilliance. An alternate reading, 'Svarna-Varna-Shesha-Pasha-Shobhitanga-Mandalam,' depicts Kalabhairava adorned with golden-colored serpents shaped like lassos.

Summary:

'I worship the main ruler of the city of Kashi, Kalabhairava, who is the upholder of the cosmic law of sustenance, dharma, who destroys unlawfulness, adharma, who liberates us from the bondage of compulsive action, karma, who bestows protection, who is of an extraordinary existence, and whose pure form radiates with the brightness of his golden flaming locks of hair!'

4.6 Shloka 6

रत्नपादुकाप्रभाभिरामपादयुग्मकं

ratnapAdukAprabhAbhirAmapAdayugmakaM

नित्यमद्वितीयमिष्टदैवतंनिरंजनम्।

nityamadvitIyamiShTadaivataMniraMjanam

मृत्युदर्पनाशनंकरालदंष्ट्रभूषणं

mRtyudarpanAshanaMkarALadaMshTrabhUShaNaM

काशिकापुराधिनाथकालभैरवंभजे॥६॥

KashikApurAdhinAthakAlabhairavaM bhaje 6

Made easy to read:

Version 1

Ratna-Paduka-Prabhabhi-Raama-Pada-Yugmakam

Nityam-Advitiyam-Ishta-Daivatam-Niramjanam

Mrtyu-Darpa-Nashanam-Karala-Damshtra-Bhushanam

Kashika-Pura-Adhinatha-Kalabhairavam-Bhaje.

Version 2:

Ratna-Paduka-Prabhabhi-Rama-Pada-Yugmakam

Nityam-Advitiyam-Istha-Daivatam-Niramjanam

Mrtyu-Darpa-Nashanam-Karala-Damshtra-Mokshanam

Kashika-Pura-Adhinatha-Kalabhairavam-Bhaje.

The first compound word in this shloka we can examine is 'Karala-Damshtra-Bhushanam.' 'Karala' means ferocious and dreadful, while 'Damshtra' refers to fangs. The term 'Bhushana' translates to ornament. Together, this compound word describes Kalabhairava as the one with fierce and dreadful fangs, likened to an adornment. Alternatively, it can be read as 'Karala-Damshtra-

Mokshanam', which means 'He who liberates us from the dreadful jaws of death.' These fearsome teeth, symbolizing death, devour all beings. Kalabhairava is portrayed as the savior who rescues us from overwhelming troubles that threaten to consume us, just as death devours life.

The next attribute, 'Mrtyu-Darpa-Nashanam', carries profound meaning. The word 'Mrtyu' literally means mortality or death and also denotes Yama, the Lord of Death. 'Darpa' translates to pride. Adi Shankaracharya ascribed pride to death because it is an inevitable constant in the life of all beings. The phrase 'Mrtyu-Darpa-Nashanam' describes Kalabhairava as the one who destroys the pride of death, for he is eternal and transcends the cycles of life and death. Kalabhairava protects his devotees from untimely death (akala mrityu) and shields them from destined death (kala mrityu), offering the wisdom that only the body perishes, while the soul (atman) is immortal.

The attribute 'Nityam' reveals Kalabhairava as eternal and constant. The term 'Dvitiyam' means second or another, but the attribute 'Adhvitiyam' signifies Kalabhairava's unparalleled nature. It highlights that he has no equal, being non-dual and inseparable from the true self, the Atman. This indicates that nothing exists apart from him or other than him.

The next attribute, 'Ishta-Devatham', translates to "the beloved deity of the devotee." The word 'Amjana' refers to dark kohl applied to the eyelashes, but it can also mean blemish. Thus, the term 'Niramjana' describes Kalabhairava as the one who is completely blemish-free.

Finally, the attribute in the first line, 'Ratna-Paduka-Prabhabhi-Rama-Pada-Yugmakam', can be broken down as follows: 'Pada-Yugmakam' means "whose pair of feet," while 'Abhirama' denotes beauty. The word 'Prabha' refers to radiance, and 'Ratna-Paduka' signifies jewel-encrusted footwear. Together, this phrase paints a vivid image of Kalabhairava as the one whose beautiful pair of feet shine with the radiance of his jeweled footwear.

Summary:

'I worship the main ruler of the city of Kashi, Kalabhairava, who is ornamented with fierce and dreadful fangs, who subdues the pride of death itself, who is constant and eternal, who is unparallelled, who is a beloved deity of worship, who is blemishless, and whose beautiful pair of feet shine with the radiance of his jewel encrusted footwear!'

4.7 Shloka 7

अट्टहासभिन्नपद्मजाण्डकोशसंततिं

aTTahAsabhinnapadmajANDakoshasaMtatiM

दृष्टिपातनष्टपापजालमुग्रशासनम्।

dRShTipAtanaShTapApajAlamugrashAsanam

अष्टसिद्धिदायकंकपालमालिकाधरं

aShTasiddhidAyakaMkapAlamAlikAdharaM

काशिकापुराधिनाथकालभैरवंभजे॥७॥

kAshikApurAdhinAthakAlabhairavaM bhaje 7

Made easy to read:

Atta-Hasa-Bhina-Padmaja-Anda-Kosha-Samtatim

Drshti-Pada-Nashta-Papa-Jalam-Ugra-Shasanam

Ashta-Siddhi-Dayakam-Kapala-Malika-Dharam

Kashika-Pura-Adhinatha-Kalabhairavam-Bhaje. 7

The term 'Kapala' literally means a skull, 'Malika' refers to a garland, and 'Dhara' signifies one who wears. Thus, 'Kapala-Malika-Dharam' portrays Kalabhairava as the one who adorns a garland of skulls. This imagery symbolizes his profound connection to death and destruction. The garland of skulls adorning Lord Kalabhairava is said to be composed of the skulls of Lord Brahma, the creator, collected by Kalabhairava at the end of each kalpa (a cosmic cycle of creation). After every kalpa, when a Brahma completes his role as the creator and passes away, it marks the inevitable dissolution of creation. Kalabhairava collects these skulls and adds them to his endless garland, representing the infinite cycles of creation and destruction he transcends.

This depiction underscores Lord Bhairava's immortality, supreme power, and his role as the eternal witness to the rise and fall of universes. It serves as a reminder that while creation is finite and bound by time, Kalabhairava exists beyond these constraints, embodying the ultimate truth of impermanence and dissolution.

The next attribute, 'Ashta-Siddhi-Dayakam,' signifies Kalabhairava as the bestower of eight divine attainments (siddhis). Here, 'Ashta' means eight, 'Siddhi' denotes powers or attainments, and 'Dayakam' refers to the giver.

Kalabhairava is described as granting these eight mystical powers to his devotees:

- ***Anima – The power to reduce one's body to the size of an atom or become invisible.***
- ***Mahima – The ability to expand one's body infinitely or become vast.***
- ***Garima – The power to become infinitely heavy and immovable.***
- ***Laghima – The ability to become extremely light or weightless.***

- ***Prapti* – *The capacity to acquire or reach anything, anywhere, at will.***
- ***Prakamya* – *The power to fulfill any desire or manifest thoughts instantly.***
- ***Ishatva* – *Absolute lordship or control over nature and material phenomena.***
- ***Vashitva* – *The ability to control or dominate all beings, including animals and people.***

Another attribute, 'Ugra-Shasanam,' depicts Kalabhairava as a fierce ruler. He guides and disciplines his devotees with unwavering authority, ensuring their steadfastness on the path of righteousness and devotion. His commands, though strict, are rooted in compassion, serving as a protective force to shield devotees from straying into wrongdoing. Even his stern punishments are expressions of boundless kindness, aimed at correcting and guiding individuals toward the right path.

The phrase 'Papa-Jalam' means "a net of sins," while 'Nashta' translates to "destroying" or "removing," and 'Drishti-Pada' refers to "the fall of a glance." The compound term 'Drishti-Pata-Nashta-Papa-Jalam' thus describes Kalabhairava as the one who can destroy the binding net of sins with just a mere glance.

Finally, the phrase forming the first line of the shloka, 'Atta-Hasa-Bhina-Padmaja-Anda-Kosha-Samtatim,' carries profound significance. Here, 'Samtatim' means a continuous happening, and 'Anda-Kosha' refers to an egg-sac, often interpreted as the source of one's birth. 'Padmaja' literally means "born out of the lotus," where the lotus symbolizes the chakras of the human body. The phrase 'Padmaja-Anda-Kosha-Samtatim' signifies the continuous series of life and death cycles arising from the chakras. The word 'Attahasa' means cacophonic laughter, and 'Bhinna' means to break or destroy.

Hence, the compound phrase describes Kalabhairava as the one who breaks the series of creations originating from the chakras with his cacophonic laughter.

At a deeper, more abstract level, these words can also symbolize the cosmic force that disrupts and dissolves the continuous cycles of life and death, leading to the ultimate dissolution of existence.

Summary :

'I worship the main ruler of the city of Kashi, Kalabhairava, who wears a series of skulls as a garland, who grants the eight great attainments, who is a fierce ruler, who destroys the binding net of sins with his mere glance, and who stops the continuous cycles of life and death, leading to ultimate liberation or mukti!'

4.8 Shloka 8

भूतसंघनायकंवशािलकीर्तदायकं

bhUtasaMghanAyakaMvishAlakIrtidAyakaM

काशविासलोकपुण्यपापशोधकंवभिुम्।

kAshivAsalokapuNyapApashodhakaMvibhum

नीतमिार्गकोवदिंपुरातनंजगत्पतिं

nItimArgakovidaMpurAtanaMjagatpatiM

काशकिापुराधनािथकालभैरवंभजे॥८॥

kAshikApurAdhinAthakAlabhairavaM bhaje 8

Made easy to read:

Bhuta-Samgha-Nayakam-Vishala-Kirti-Dayakam

Kashi-Vasa-Loka-Punya-Papa-Shodhakam-Vibhum

Niti-Marga-Kovidam-Puratanam-Jagatpatim

Kashika-Pura-Adhinatha-Kalabhairavam-Bhaje. 8

The term 'Bhuta' refers to both departed spirits and the primordial elements of creation. The word 'Samgha' means a group, while 'Nayaka' denotes a leader. Together, the attribute 'Bhuta-Samgha-Nayakam' signifies that Kalabhairava is the leader of both the departed spirits and the five elements of creation.

In the next attribute, 'Vishala-Kirti-Dayakam,' 'Vishala' means vast and widespread, 'Kirti' represents fame or reputation, and 'Dayaka' refers to the one who bestows. Thus, 'Vishala-Kirti-dayakam' portrays Kalabhairava as the granter of widespread fame.

The attribute 'Kashi-Vasa-Loka-Punya-Papa-Shodhakam' is next. Here, the word 'Shodhana,' derived from the same root as 'Shuddhi,' means to purify or cleanse. This describes Kalabhairava as the one who purifies both the vices (Papa) and virtues (Punya) of those residing in Kashi.

The word 'Vibhum' depicts Kalabhairava as one with an extraordinary existence.

The term 'Kovida' refers to an expert, while 'Marga' means path, and 'Niti' signifies righteousness. The phrase 'Niti-Marga-Kovidam' illustrates Kalabhairava as an expert in following and guiding others along the path of righteousness. Next, the word 'Puratanam' means ancient, and 'Jagat-Patim' translates to the lord of the entire world. Together, the attribute 'Puratanamjagatpatim' describes Kalabhairava as both ancient and the lord of all worlds.

Summary:

'I worship the main ruler of the city of Kashi, Kalabhairava, who is the leader of the bhUtas, who grants wide-spread fame, who cleanses the vices and virtues of the residents of Kashi, who is of an extraordinary existence, who is an expert in the path of righteousness, who is ancient, and who is the lord of the entire world!'

4.9. Phalashruthi

कालभैरवाष्टकंपठंतयिमनोहरं

kAlabhairavAsh TakaM paThaMti ye manoharaM

ज्ञानमुक्तसािधनंवचितित्रपुण्यवर्धनम्।

jnAnamuktisAdhanaMvichitrapuNyavardhanam

शोकमोहदैन्यलोभकोपतापनाशनं

shokamohadainyalobhakopatApanAshanaM

प्रयान्तकिालभैरवांघ्रसिन्नधिनिराध्रुवम्॥

prayAntikAlabhairavAMghrisannidhiMnarAdhruvam

Made easy to read:

Kalabhairava-Ashtakam-Pathanti-Ye-Manoharam

Jnana-Mukti-Sadhanam-Vicitra-Punya-Vardhanam

Shoka-Moha-Dainya-Lobha-Kopa-Tapa-Nashanam

Prayanti-Kalabhairava-Angri-Sanidhim-Nara-Dhruvam. 9

The Phala Shruti (verse describing the benefits of recitation) of the Kalabhairava Ashtakam is a significant addition, though it is not officially a part of the main ashtakam. Reciting it is optional and not a compulsion alongside the eight official stanzas.

According to the Phala Shruti, those who chant (ye pathanti) this beautiful (manoharam) composition in praise of Lord Kalabhairava (Kalabhairava Ashtakam) are blessed with knowledge (jnana) and liberation (mukti). The recitation also enhances the sadhaka's life with various virtuous qualities (vicitra punya vardhanam). Moreover, it is said to destroy grief (shoka), delusion (moha), pitifulness (dainya), greed (lobha), rage (kopa), and despair (tapa). Such devoted individuals (nara-dhruvam) are assured of attaining the divine abode at the feet of Kalabhairava (Kalabhairava-anghri-sanidhim).

4.10 Concluding Shloka

॥इतश्रि्रीमत्परमहंसपरव्रि्राजकाचर्यस्य

itishrImatparamahaMsaparivrAjakAchAryasya

श्रीगोवन्दिभगवत्पूज्यपादशष्यिस्यश्रीमच्छङ्करभगवतकृतौ

shrIgovindabhagavatpUjyapAdashiShyasyashrImach

Chankarabhagavata HkRtau

श्रीकालभैरवाष्टकंसम्पूरणम्॥

shrIkAlabhairavAShTakaMsampUrNam

Made easy to read:

Iti Shrimad-Paramahamsa-Parivrajakacharyasya

Shri-Govinda-Bhagavat-Pujya-Pada-Shishyasya

Shrimach-ChankarabhagavatahKritau

Shri Kalabhairav-Ashtakam Sampurnam.

Thus, the auspicious Kalabhairava ashtakam among the compositions of Shrimat Shankaracharya, a wandering enlightened mystic, and the disciple of Shri Govinda Bhagavatpada, is complete!

5

BENEFITS OF RECITING KALABHAIRAVA ASHTAKAM

Reciting the Kalabhairava Ashtakam offers transformative benefits that span spiritual, psychological, and practical dimensions. At its core, the hymn invokes Kalabhairava, a fierce form of Lord Shiva, who is the protector of time, destroyer of fear, and guardian of righteousness. One of the most profound benefits of this recitation is the removal of fear and negativity. Kalabhairava's divine presence instills a deep sense of courage, empowering devotees to face life's challenges with resilience. The chant is believed to create an energetic shield that protects against negative influences, unseen dangers, and harmful energies.

The hymn also addresses one of the fundamental obstacles in spiritual growth: the ego. By reciting the Kalabhairava Ashtakam, devotees reflect on the transient nature of life and the futility of material attachments. This practice gradually dissolves ignorance and arrogance, fostering humility and a deeper understanding of life's higher purpose. The verses remind devotees that the ultimate goal is liberation (moksha), encouraging them to transcend worldly desires and align with eternal truths. Kalabhairava, as the Lord of Time (Kala), urges devotees to respect time and live with discipline. Regular recitation inspires mindfulness, better time management, and a sense of urgency to focus on righteous actions and spiritual progress.

In addition to spiritual benefits, the hymn has a calming effect on the mind. Its rhythmic chanting soothes anxiety, alleviates stress, and fosters emotional stability. Devotees often experience mental clarity and a strengthened resolve to face challenges. Kalabhairava is also revered as a cosmic protector, and the recitation of his Ashtakam invokes his guidance and blessings. His protective energy is believed to remove obstacles, protect from harm, and help devotees navigate life's uncertainties. This makes the hymn particularly powerful for those seeking strength and assurance during difficult times.

Beyond protection, the Kalabhairava Ashtakam is associated with material and spiritual prosperity. Devotees often turn to the hymn to remove barriers to success, gain clarity in decision-making, and invite stability into their lives. The hymn is also a source of inspiration, awakening inner strength and self-confidence. By meditating on Kalabhairava's fierce yet compassionate form, devotees find the courage to confront adversities and grow stronger from their experiences.

On a cosmic level, Kalabhairava is seen as the force that maintains universal order. Reciting his hymn aligns devotees with this divine energy, fostering harmony within and around them. This alignment helps create a balanced life, where spiritual aspirations and worldly responsibilities coexist seamlessly. The Kalabhairava Ashtakam is, therefore, more than a devotional practice—it is a journey of self-transformation. It inspires fearlessness, discipline, and spiritual clarity, ultimately guiding devotees toward peace, prosperity, and liberation. Through its sacred verses, the hymn connects the reciter with the eternal truths of time, courage, and divine grace.

6

SYMBOLISM OF KALABHAIRAVA

Figure 2: *Kalabhairava*

His terrifying form, with dark complexion, blazing eyes, and a garland of skulls, signifies the destruction of negativity and the impermanence of life. Each of his weapons carries deep meaning: the trident (trishula) destroys impurities and represents control over time; the drum (damaru) reflects the rhythmic cycle of creation and destruction; the sword cuts through illusions, and the skull (kapala) symbolizes the transient nature of physical existence. Together, these attributes emphasize the need to rise above attachments and focus on spiritual truth.

Kalabhairava's vehicle, the black dog, represents loyalty, protection, and the ability to navigate life's darkness. Feeding dogs is considered an act of reverence to him. His four arms and omnipresence across the directions symbolize his mastery over the cosmic order, ensuring balance, justice, and protection. The garland of skulls he wears further reminds devotees of life's fleeting nature and the importance of seeking the eternal soul.

As the "Kotwal" or guardian of sacred cities like Kashi and Ujjain, Kalabhairava ensures their spiritual sanctity. In the broader sense, he protects the moral and spiritual order of the universe, guiding devotees toward liberation. He plays a crucial role at the time of death, freeing those who surrender to him from the cycle of birth and death. Kalabhairava's eight forms (Ashta Bhairava) represent various aspects of existence and cosmic forces, offering devotees deeper insights into life and spiritual alignment.

Kalabhairava's teachings remind us of the impermanence of life and the importance of fearlessness, self-discipline, and respect for time. His symbolism urges us to confront challenges with courage, overcome attachments to the material world, and focus on the eternal truth, ultimately leading to liberation (moksha). Through his awe-inspiring presence, Kalabhairava guides us toward wisdom, transformation, and spiritual freedom.

7

THE EIGHT FORMS OF KALABHAIRAVA

Kalabhairava, a fierce and protective form of Lord Shiva, manifests in eight primary forms called the Ashta Bhairavas. Each form represents different aspects of creation, preservation, and destruction. These forms symbolize the control over the eight directions of the earth, offering protection and spiritual growth. Below is a simple explanation of each form:

1. Asitanga Bhairava

- Direction: East
- Attributes: Represents creation and purity.
- Symbolism: Encourages spiritual beginnings and pursuit of truth.
- Association: Jupiter, symbolizing wisdom and knowledge.
- Vehicle: Swan
- Consort: Brahmani
- Complexion: White
- Weapons: Japamala, kamandala, sword, skull cup
- Shrine: Sattainathar Temple, Sirkazhi; Kandeeswarar Temple, Kandiyur
- Asterism: Pushya
- Deity: Vishnu

2. Ruru Bhairava

- Direction: Southeast
- Attributes: Embodies knowledge, wisdom, and music.
- Symbolism: Guides seekers on the path of learning and creative arts.
- Association: Venus, symbolizing beauty and harmony.
- Vehicle: Bull
- Consort: Maheshvari
- Complexion: Light blue
- Weapons: Deer, axe, sword, bowl
- Shrine: Rathnagiriswarar Temple, Thirumarugal
- Asterism: Krttika, Uttara Ashadha, Uttara Phalguni
- Deity: Brahma

3. Chanda Bhairava

- Direction: South
- Attributes: Represents strength, courage, and intense energy.
- Symbolism: Helps overcome fear and obstacles in life.
- Association: Mars, linked to aggression and assertiveness.
- Vehicle: Peacock
- Consort: Kaumari
- Complexion: White
- Weapons: Bow, arrow, sword, bowl
- Shrine: Vaitheeswaran Koil
- Asterism: Mrigashirsha, Chitra, Dhanishta
- Deity: Surya

4. Krodha Bhairava

- Direction: Southwest
- Attributes: Embodies anger and righteous indignation.
- Symbolism: Protects devotees by destroying evil and injustice.
- Association: Saturn, linked to discipline and transformation.
- Vehicle: Eagle
- Consort: Vaishnavi
- Complexion: Dark blue
- Weapons: Conch, discus, mace, bowl
- Shrine: Thiruvisanallur, Thirunaraiyur
- Asterism: Rohini, Hasta, Shravana
- Deity: Shiva

5. Unmatta Bhairava

- Direction: West
- Attributes: Symbolizes divine madness and detachment.
- Symbolism: Liberates one from ego and worldly attachments.
- Association: Mercury, representing intellect and clarity.
- Vehicle: Horse
- Consort: Varahi
- Complexion: Golden
- Weapons: Sword, skull cup, pestle, shield
- Shrine: Thiruveezhimizhalai

- Asterism: Punarvasu, Vishakha, Anuradha, Purva Bhadrapada, Uttara Bhadrapada
- Deity: Indra

6. Kapala Bhairava

- Direction: Northwest
- Attributes: Associated with rituals, spirituality, and offerings.
- Symbolism: Grants blessings and spiritual prosperity.
- Association: Moon, representing the mind and emotions.
- Vehicle: Elephant
- Consort: Indrani
- Complexion: Shining yellow
- Weapons: Thunderbolt, noose, sword, bowl
- Shrine: Thiruvirkudi, Pushpavaneswarar Temple
- Asterism: Bharani, Purva Ashadha, Purva Phalguni
- Deity: Chandra

7. Bhisana Bhairava

- Direction: North
- Attributes: Represents terror and awe.
- Symbolism: Scares away negative energies and protects devotees.
- Association: Ketu, representing detachment and spiritual insight.
- Vehicle: Preta

- Consort: Chamunda
- Complexion: Blood red
- Weapons: Sword, skull cup, trident, pestle
- Shrine: Rameswaram, Piranmalai
- Asterism: Ardra, Svati, Shatabhisha, Ashvini, Magha, Mula
- Deity: Yama

8. Samhara Bhairava

- Direction: Northeast
- Attributes: The ultimate destroyer of ignorance and illusion.
- Symbolism: Assists in liberation (moksha) and spiritual enlightenment.
- Association: Rahu, representing hidden fears and shadows.
- Vehicle: Lion
- Consort: Pratyangira
- Complexion: Lightning-yellow-orange
- Weapons: Trident, drum, conch, mace, discus, sword, bowl, skull-topped staff, noose, goad
- Shrine: Thiruvenkadu, Kolli Hills, Vairavanpatti, Hosur
- Asterism: Ashlesha, Jyeshtha, Revati
- Deity: Shiva

Figure 3: *Kalabhairava with Astha Bhairavas*

The 64 Forms of Kalabhairava

The Ashta Bhairavas are expanded into 64 forms of Kalabhairava (Chausath Bhairavas). Each form represents a unique aspect of Lord Shiva's energy and is worshiped for specific purposes.

Key Themes Among the 64 Forms:

- Protection: Many forms act as guardians, warding off evil spirits and misfortune.
- Knowledge: Several forms provide wisdom and clarity for spiritual and worldly challenges.
- Wealth: Some forms are worshiped to attract prosperity and success.
- Justice: Kalabhairava's forms ensure justice and the punishment of wrongdoers.
- Time Management: He is the lord of time (Kala), reminding devotees to use their time wisely.
- Liberation: Many forms guide seekers toward freedom from the cycle of birth and death.

Some of the forms are listed below:

- Swarnaakarshana Bhairava: Attracts wealth and removes poverty.
- Kala Bhairava: Manages time and aids in spiritual discipline.
- Roudra Bhairava: Destroys enemies and grants protection.
- Bheema Bhairava: Provides immense strength and courage.
- Ananda Bhairava: Offers joy and peace of mind.

Each form is worshiped with specific rituals and offerings, often tailored to the needs of the devotee. The diversity in Kalabhairava's forms reflects his universal nature, encompassing all aspects of life and the cosmos.

8

CONCEPT OF KALA IN SANATANA DHARMA

In Sanatana Dharma, Kala (time) is not merely a chronological measure of moments but a cosmic principle that governs the rhythm of existence. It is considered one of the fundamental realities of the universe, intrinsically linked to the processes of creation (Srishti), preservation (Sthiti), and destruction (Pralaya). Unlike the linear progression of time commonly understood in Western thought, Kala is cyclical in nature, reflecting the repetitive and eternal cycles of birth, death, and rebirth. This cyclical understanding is embodied in the concept of the Yugas—Satya Yuga, Treta Yuga, Dvapara Yuga, and Kali Yuga—which collectively form a Maha Yuga of 4.32 million years. These cycles repeat endlessly, symbolizing the infinite nature of time.

At a deeper level, Kala is viewed as an expression of the divine. The Bhagavad Gita illustrates this when Lord Krishna, as the embodiment of the Supreme Consciousness, declares, "I am Time, the great destroyer of the world" (Kalosmilokakshayakritpravriddho). This statement underscores the omnipotent and all-encompassing nature of Kala, which governs not only the physical universe but also the destinies of all beings. It serves as a humbling reminder of the transient nature of material existence and the inevitability of change.

In the context of Hindu cosmology, Kala is intricately tied to the Trimurti—the three principal deities of creation, preservation, and destruction. Brahma operates within the framework of time to create, Vishnu sustains creation through the ages, and Shiva, in his form as Mahakala or Kalabhairava, transcends and annihilates time, symbolizing the dissolution necessary for rebirth. Among these, Shiva's aspect as Kalabhairava is especially significant. As the "Lord of Time," Kalabhairava represents the ultimate truth that time controls all, yet the divine essence exists beyond its grasp, offering liberation (Moksha) from the bondage of temporal existence.

Philosophically, Kala is also tied to the doctrine of Karma. Every action performed within the bounds of time has consequences, shaping the future experiences of the soul. This interplay of Kala and Karma emphasizes the importance of living a righteous life in alignment with Dharma, as time provides both the arena and the impetus for spiritual evolution.

Furthermore, Kala is not seen as a mere adversary or destroyer; it is also seen as a teacher. It teaches patience, impermanence, and the importance of focusing on eternal truths rather than ephemeral desires. By meditating on Kala as a cosmic force, individuals are encouraged to transcend the illusions of the material world and connect with the unchanging reality of the Self (Atman) and the ultimate reality of Brahman.

In this way, Kala in Sanatana Dharma is a multifaceted concept—a relentless force, a divine principle, and a spiritual guide—encouraging a holistic understanding of life, the universe, and the journey toward liberation. It is both the cycle of existence and the key to transcending it.

9

WORSHIP OF KALABHAIRAVA

Worshiping Kalabhairava involves devotion, discipline, and adherence to certain rituals. Here are general guidelines and rituals commonly followed:

General Rules

- Purity: Maintain physical and mental purity. Take a bath and wear clean clothes before beginning the puja.
- Timings: Worship Kalabhairava ideally during midnight, on a Sunday or Tuesday, or on Ashtami Tithi (eighth lunar day).
- Direction: Face the North or East while performing the puja.
- Devotional Mindset: Approach the deity with humility, devotion, and a clear heart, as Kalabhairava symbolizes justice and time.
- Cleanliness of Space: Ensure the worship area is clean and sanctified.

Rituals for Kalabhairava Worship

- **Altar Preparation**
  Place an idol or image of Kalabhairava on a clean, sacred platform.

Adorn the idol with garlands of flowers like hibiscus and lotus.

Light a diya (oil lamp) using mustard oil to create a purified and sacred atmosphere.

- **Offerings (Naivedya)**
  Offer black sesame seeds, urad dal, coconuts, bananas, and jaggery-based sweets.

  In certain tantric traditions, liquor may also be offered. Ensure offerings align with your beliefs and practices.

  Light incense sticks and offer a diya (oil lamp) along with these offerings.

- **Mantras and Stotras**
  Chant the Kalabhairava Ashtakam to invoke his blessings.

  Recite the following powerful mantras:
  "Om Bhairavaya Namaha"

  "Om Kaal Bhairavaya Namaha"

- **Abhishekam (Sacred Bath)**
  Perform Abhishekam to the idol using water, milk, honey, yogurt, and ghee.

  Follow with a rinse using clean water, symbolizing purification.

- **Aarti and Bhajan**
  Conclude the puja with an Aarti dedicated to Kalabhairava.

  Offer incense and a camphor flame while chanting mantras or devotional songs in his honor.

- **Circumambulation (Pradakshina)**
  Perform eight rounds (Pradakshina) around the idol or image, symbolizing the eight forms of Bhairava.

- **Feeding Dogs**
  Kalabhairava is associated with dogs, which are regarded as his divine vehicle.

  Feeding dogs is believed to be highly auspicious and a sign of devotion.

- **Charity and Acts of Kindness**
  Offer donations to the poor or support religious activities as an expression of generosity, pleasing Kalabhairava.

Things to Avoid

- Negative Emotions: Avoid anger, greed, and jealousy during worship.
- Impurity: Avoid performing the puja without a proper bath or in an unclean space.
- Disrespect to Time: Kalabhairava represents time (Kaal). Be punctual and disciplined.

By worshiping Kalabhairava with sincerity and devotion, devotees seek protection, justice, spiritual growth, and liberation from fear and negativity.

10

KALABHAIRAVA AND KASHI

Kashi, also known as Varanasi, holds a unique place in Indian spirituality as one of the oldest living cities in the world and as a center of learning, culture, and devotion. Its significance is deeply rooted in Sanatana Dharma, with Lord Shiva being its presiding deity. Among Shiva's many forms, Kalabhairava is regarded as the fierce guardian of Kashi. He is known as the "Kotwal" or the protector of the city and its cosmic order.

Kalabhairava and Kashi's Eternal Connection

Kashi is not just a geographical location; it is believed to be a divine field where the soul attains liberation. Scriptures describe Kashi as a place that exists in both the material and spiritual planes. It is said that the city was personally established by Lord Shiva, who declared it his eternal abode.

Kalabhairava serves as the divine guardian of Kashi. According to tradition, no one can reside or leave Kashi without his permission. Even death within Kashi is said to be under his jurisdiction. The Kashi Khanda of the Skanda Purana mentions that when a person dies in Kashi, Kalabhairava ensures that their soul is freed from the cycle of birth and death.

The significance of Kalabhairava in Kashi is beautifully illustrated through the ritual of Kapala Mochana. According to legend, Lord Shiva created Kalabhairava to decapitate Brahma's fifth head, which had become a source of arrogance. After completing this task, Kalabhairava was cursed to carry the skull as a penance. He wandered across many sacred places but was finally freed from the burden when he arrived in Kashi. Hence, Kashi became known as a place of ultimate liberation, and Kalabhairava was established as its eternal protector.

The Worship of Kalabhairava

Kalabhairava is venerated through a sacred ritual called Bhairava Ashtami, celebrated on the eighth day of the waning moon in the month of Margashirsha. On this day, devotees offer prayers, light lamps, and chant the Kalabhairava Ashtakam, a hymn praising his divine qualities.

The most famous temple dedicated to Kalabhairava is the Kalabhairava Temple in Varanasi, where devotees seek his blessings for courage, success, and spiritual wisdom. It is customary to offer black sesame seeds, oil lamps, and mustard oil at the temple. Devotees also feed dogs, regarded as Kalabhairava's sacred vahana (vehicle), as an act of reverence.

Figure 4: *Kalabhairava Temple, Varanasi*

Spiritual Lessons from Kalabhairava and Kashi

Kalabhairava teaches us the impermanence of life and the importance of time. Kashi, as his eternal abode, reminds us to rise above worldly attachments and seek spiritual truth. Together, they inspire a path of devotion, self-discipline, and the pursuit of liberation.

In Kashi, where the Ganga flows and spirituality pervades every corner, Kalabhairava stands as a timeless guardian, guiding souls toward the ultimate goal—freedom from the cycle of birth and death.

11

KALABHAIRAVA AND UJJAIN

Ujjain, one of the most ancient and sacred cities of India, holds profound spiritual and historical significance. It is renowned for its association with Lord Shiva and is considered one of the seven holy cities (Sapta Moksha Puris) in Sanatana Dharma. Among Ujjain's many divine connections, the worship of Kalabhairava stands out as a significant aspect of the city's spiritual identity.

In Ujjain, Kalabhairava is not only a deity but also the city's cosmic guardian, protecting its spiritual sanctity. His presence signifies the balance between creation and destruction, urging devotees to respect the flow of time and live righteously.

The Kalabhairava Temple in Ujjain

The Kalabhairava Temple in Ujjain is one of the most famous shrines dedicated to this formidable deity. Located on the banks of the Shipra River, it is a major pilgrimage site and a key attraction for spiritual seekers.

The temple's origins are ancient, dating back to the Paramara Dynasty, and it has been an important center of tantric practices. The architecture reflects a blend of artistry and devotion, with intricate carvings and an atmosphere charged with spiritual energy.

The most unique and intriguing ritual at the Kalabhairava Temple is the offering of liquor. Devotees present liquor to the deity as naivedya (offering), which is then poured into the mouth of the deity's idol. This tradition, which may seem unconventional, is deeply rooted in tantric practices and symbolizes surrender to the divine.

Ujjain: The City of Time

Ujjain is also known as Avantika and Mahakal ki Nagari (the city of Lord Mahakal, another form of Shiva). It is home to the famous Mahakaleshwar Jyotirlinga, one of the twelve sacred Jyotirlingas of Shiva. Kalabhairava and Mahakal are closely connected, as both represent Shiva's control over time and death.

The city's association with time is further emphasized by its historical role as an important center for astronomy and astrology. The ancient Indian concept of timekeeping, including the measurement of planetary movements, was developed here. Ujjain is believed to be the Greenwich of Hindu astronomy, and Kalabhairava is regarded as the eternal custodian of cosmic time.

The Legend of Kalabhairava in Ujjain

According to local lore, Ujjain was once ruled by demon kings who disrupted the spiritual order. To restore balance, Lord Shiva manifested as Kalabhairava and vanquished the demons, establishing peace and dharma in the region. This victory cemented Kalabhairava's role as the protector of Ujjain.

Another legend relates to Shiva's Rudra Tandava, the dance of cosmic destruction. It is said that Kalabhairava emerged from Shiva during this dance, tasked with maintaining cosmic harmony. His presence in Ujjain serves as a reminder of Shiva's power to create, protect, and dissolve the universe.

Ujjain, Kalabhairava, and Moksha

Ujjain, with its divine aura and association with Kalabhairava, represents the interplay of time and eternity. Kalabhairava reminds us of the impermanence of life and the need to align our actions with higher spiritual goals. For those seeking liberation (moksha), Ujjain serves as a gateway, where the grace of Kalabhairava helps transcend the limitations of time and attain eternal peace.

Through his divine presence, Kalabhairava continues to protect and bless Ujjain, guiding seekers on their journey toward self-realization and liberation.

12

FAMOUS TEMPLES OF KALABHAIRAVA

Kalabhairava is venerated as a fierce and protective deity across India, and many temples are dedicated to him. These temples not only hold religious significance but also reflect the rich cultural and spiritual heritage associated with Kalabhairava worship. Here are some of the most famous Kalabhairava temples:

- **Kalabhairava Temple, Kashi (Varanasi, Uttar Pradesh)**
  Located in the sacred city of Varanasi, this temple is one of the most prominent Kalabhairava shrines in India.Kalabhairava is regarded as the "Kotwal" (guardian deity) of Kashi, and visiting this temple is considered essential to completing a pilgrimage to Varanasi.The temple holds deep spiritual significance and attracts countless devotees seeking his protection and blessings.

- **Kalabhairava Temple, Ujjain (Madhya Pradesh)**
  One of the most famous Kalabhairava temples, located in the holy city of Ujjain, associated with the Mahakaleshwar Jyotirlinga.Known for its unique tradition where devotees offer liquor as a part of worship.The temple attracts thousands of devotees seeking protection and blessings.

- **Sri Kalabhairaveshwara Swamy Temple, Adichunchanagiri (Karnataka)**

  Situated in Mandya district, this temple is a major pilgrimage center for followers of Lord Kalabhairava.

  It is associated with the Adichunchanagiri Mutt, a significant spiritual institution in Karnataka.

- **Bhairav Nath Temple, Bhairav Ghati (Uttarakhand)**

  Situated near the Kedarnath Temple, this temple honors Bhairava as the guardian of the Kedarnath shrine.

  Devotees often visit this temple after completing their pilgrimage to Kedarnath.

- **Kala Bhairava Temple, Kathmandu (Nepal)**

  This historic temple is situated in Hanuman Dhoka Durbar Square, a UNESCO World Heritage Site.The deity is revered as the protector of the city, and the temple is an important center for Hindu and Buddhist worship.

- **Kalabhairava Temple, Bhubaneswar (Odisha)**

  Located in the ancient city of Bhubaneswar, this temple reflects the influence of Shaivism in Odisha's spiritual tradition. Devotees seek Kalabhairava's blessings for protection and resolution of hardships.

- **Kala Bhairava Temple, Chennai (Tamil Nadu)**

  Situated in Puzhal, this temple is dedicated to Kalabhairava and is particularly popular during Ashtami, the eighth day of the lunar cycle.The deity is worshipped for overcoming obstacles and gaining success.

- **Shri Kalabhairaveshwara Swamy Temple, Kallidaikurichi (Tamil Nadu)**
  Located near Tirunelveli, this ancient temple is an important pilgrimage spot for devotees of Kalabhairava.Known for its serene environment and significant spiritual energy.

- **Kalabhairava Temples in Himachal Pradesh**
  Several Kalabhairava temples are located in the hill state, including ones near Jwalamukhi and Chintpurni.

These temples are often part of broader pilgrimage circuits dedicated to Devi and Shiva.

These temples highlight Kalabhairava's enduring significance as a deity who protects, empowers, and guides his devotees. They also stand as architectural and cultural marvels, embodying centuries of devotion and tradition.

13

TIMELESS WISDOM OF KALABHAIRAVA: RELEVANCE OF THE KALABHAIRAVA ASHTAKAM IN THE MODERN WORLD

The Kalabhairava Ashtakam and the concept of Kalabhairava are profoundly relevant to the contemporary world, offering timeless spiritual insights and practical wisdom. Kalabhairava, as the "Lord of Time," symbolizes mastery over time and reminds us to prioritize what truly matters in our fast-paced lives. The Ashtakam emphasizes the transient nature of life, urging mindfulness and living in the present moment—essential principles for managing stress and achieving personal growth.

Kalabhairava's fierce form represents the courage to confront and overcome fears, such as fear of death, failure, or uncertainty. In an age rife with anxiety and existential challenges, his worship provides strength and resilience. Chanting the Kalabhairava Ashtakam instills fearlessness and helps navigate life's crises with confidence. The hymn also highlights the importance of discipline and devotion in spiritual practice, reminding us to reconnect with the divine and our higher purpose amidst the distractions of materialism.

Kalabhairava is also revered as a protector for travelers and metaphorically for those on mental and emotional journeys, offering stability in uncertain times. Meditating on or reciting the Ashtakam creates a psychological sense of safety, fostering inner strength and clarity. Furthermore, Kalabhairava's association with breaking illusions and guiding devotees toward enlightenment is particularly relevant in an era dominated by misinformation and superficial pursuits. His energy inspires the pursuit of truth, self-awareness, and detachment from ego-driven illusions.

Temples dedicated to Kalabhairava continue to draw seekers interested in tantra, meditation, and transformative practices, demonstrating his enduring significance. For modern practitioners, the Kalabhairava Ashtakam serves as a meditative tool to align with cosmic rhythms and cultivate inner peace. In essence, the teachings of Kalabhairava address universal human challenges and provide spiritual tools to lead balanced, fearless, and purposeful lives in today's world.

14

ADI SHANKARACHARYA

14.1. Who is Adi Shankaracharya?

Adi Shankara, also known as Adi Shankaracharya, is one of the greatest philosophers and spiritual teachers in Indian history. He lived during the 8th century CE and is best known for reviving and spreading Advaita Vedanta, a philosophy that teaches the oneness of the soul (Atman) with the ultimate reality (Brahman). His teachings and works have a lasting influence on Hinduism, spirituality, and Indian culture.

Figure 5: *Adi Shankaracharya*

Early Life of Adi Shankara

Adi Shankara was born in a small village called Kaladi in present-day Kerala, India. His parents, Shivaguru and Aryamba, were devout Brahmins who had long prayed for a child. Their prayers were answered, and Shankara was born as a blessing from Lord Shiva.From a very young age, Shankara showed extraordinary intelligence and spiritual inclination. By the age of three, he could recite scriptures, and by seven, he had mastered the Vedas (ancient sacred texts). His mother greatly influenced his spiritual growth, and even as a child, he showed signs of being a great thinker and teacher.

Becoming a Monk

Shankara lost his father at a young age, an event that deeply impacted his life, inspiring his quest for spiritual knowledge and truth. However, his mother, deeply attached to him, wanted him to lead a normal life, free from the responsibilities of renunciation and worldly duties.

One day, while bathing in the Purna River, a crocodile suddenly seized Shankara's leg and began dragging him into the water. In great distress, he cried out to his mother, asking for permission to become a sannyasi (monk), as the crocodile had promised to release him if she agreed. Despite her deep affection for her only son and her reluctance to let him go, his mother, torn between love and duty, ultimately gave her consent, trusting in his spiritual calling. Hearing her permission, the crocodile released Shankara, who then left home to embark on his journey as a wandering monk, devoted to the pursuit of spiritual wisdom and enlightenment.

Shankara's Spiritual Journey

Shankara wandered across India, seeking a guru. He eventually found Sri Govindapada, a great sage, and became his disciple. Under his guidance, Shankara learned about Advaita Vedanta, a philosophy that teaches that the soul (Atman) and the universal reality (Brahman) are one and the same.After completing his studies, Shankara started traveling across India to spread this knowledge. During his travels, he debated with scholars of different philosophical schools, such as Buddhism, Jainism, and other branches of Hinduism. His deep wisdom and logical arguments convinced many people of the truth of Advaita Vedanta.

Teachings of Adi Shankara

Adi Shankara's main teaching was Advaita Vedanta, which means "non-dualism." This philosophy explains that:

- The ultimate reality, called Brahman, is formless, eternal, and infinite.
- The individual soul, or Atman, is not different from Brahman; they are one and the same.
- The world we see around us is maya, or illusion. It feels real because of ignorance, but true wisdom reveals that everything is Brahman.

Shankara taught that the goal of life is to overcome ignorance, realize the oneness of Atman and Brahman, and attain liberation (moksha).

14.2 Contribution of Adi Shankaracharya to Sanatana Dharma

Adi Shankaracharya, one of the most revered philosophers and theologians in Indian history, played a pivotal role in the revival, consolidation, and propagation of Sanatana Dharma. His contributions are profound and multifaceted, influencing philosophy, spirituality, culture, and religious practices. Here is a detailed account of his contributions:

- **Advaita Vedanta Philosophy**

Adi Shankara is best known for formalizing and propagating Advaita Vedanta (Non-dualism), which teaches the oneness of the individual soul (Atman) with the ultimate reality (Brahman). His teachings challenged dualistic and materialistic philosophies, emphasizing that:

The world is ultimately an illusion (Maya). The realization of one's unity with Brahman leads to liberation (Moksha).

Knowledge (Jnana) is the primary means to achieve liberation, as opposed to mere rituals.This philosophy became the cornerstone of Sanatana Dharma and provided a unifying framework for spiritual seekers.

- **Bhashyas (Commentaries on Scriptures)**

Shankara wrote extensive commentaries (Bhashyas) on foundational texts of Sanatana Dharma, clarifying their meanings and harmonizing diverse schools of thought. These include:

  * Brahmasutras: His Brahmasutra Bhashya is the definitive Advaita Vedanta interpretation.
  * Principal Upanishads: He commented on 10 major Upanishads, elucidating their non-dualistic essence.
  * Bhagavad Gita: His commentary on the Gita highlights the harmony between Jnana (knowledge), Bhakti (devotion), and Karma (action).

These works re-established the scriptural basis for Advaita Vedanta and countered interpretations from other schools.

- **Unification of Sanatana Dharma**

During Shankara's time, there was significant fragmentation within Hinduism due to the rise of heterodox sects (e.g., Buddhism and Jainism) and internal conflicts. He unified Sanatana Dharma by:

* Reconciling divergent practices and philosophies, demonstrating how they all lead to the same ultimate truth.
* Establishing the supremacy of Vedic teachings as the foundation of Hindu philosophy.
* Declaring that the essence of worship and spirituality is the realization of Brahman, irrespective of the deity or practice followed.

- **Establishment of Mathas (Monastic Institutions)**

Shankara established four principal Mathas (monasteries) in the cardinal directions of India to preserve and propagate Vedantic teachings:

- Sringeri (South): Associated with the Yajur Veda.
- Dwaraka (West): Associated with the Sama Veda.
- Puri (East): Associated with the Rig Veda.
- Joshimath (North): Associated with the Atharva Veda.

These institutions became centers of learning and spirituality, playing a crucial role in preserving Sanatana Dharma for generations.

- **Panchayatana Puja System**

Shankara introduced the Panchayatana Puja system to unify diverse sects, integrating the worship of five principal deities. Shiva, Vishnu, Devi, Surya, and Ganesha.This inclusive system demonstrated that all deities are manifestations of the same ultimate reality (Brahman), fostering harmony among different sects.

- **Countering Non-Vedic Philosophies**

Adi Shankara was instrumental in countering the dominance of Buddhism and other heterodox systems that had overshadowed

Vedic traditions. Through debates with Buddhist scholars like Mandana Mishra, he demonstrated the relevance and logical soundness of Vedantic philosophy, leading to the re-establishment of Vedic authority.

- **Compositions and Hymns**

Shankara composed numerous devotional hymns that combined profound philosophy with deep devotion, making spiritual truths accessible to common people. These include:

  - Bhaja Govindam: Encouraging the pursuit of spiritual knowledge over material pursuits.
  - Saundarya Lahari: Celebrating the divine feminine and the beauty of devotion.
  - Vivekachudamani: A philosophical treatise on discernment and the path to liberation.

Other hymns on Shiva, Vishnu, and Devicontinue to inspire devotion and faith.

- **Integration of Bhakti and Jnana**

Shankara emphasized that Jnana (knowledge) and Bhakti (devotion) are not contradictory but complementary. His hymns and teachings demonstrated that devotion is a valid and powerful path to realizing Brahman alongside intellectual inquiry.

- **Promotion of Ethical Living and Dharma**

Shankara's teachings highlighted the importance of living a life rooted in Dharma (righteousness) as a prerequisite for spiritual growth. His guidance on ethical conduct and self-discipline remain central to Sanatana Dharma.

- **Legacy**

Shankara's influence on Sanatana Dharma is unparalleled. His works laid the foundation for subsequent schools of Vedanta and philosophical thought. He ensured the survival and resurgence of Vedic traditions during a time of crisis, and his legacy continues to shape Hindu philosophy, spirituality, and culture.

In summary, Adi Shankaracharya's life was dedicated to reviving, unifying, and enriching Sanatana Dharma, leaving a timeless legacy that guides seekers across the world.

KALABHAIRAVA ASHTAKAM

Devaraja-Sevyamana-Pavana-Angri-Pankajam,
Vyala-Yagna-Suthram-Indu-Shekaram-Krupakaram,
Naradadhi-Yogi-Vrundha-Vandhitham-Digambaram,
Kasika-Pura-Adhinatha-Kalabhairavam-Bhaje. 1

Bhanu-Koti-Bhasvaram-Bhavabdhi-Tarakam-Param
Nila-Kantham-Iipsita-Artha-Dayakam-Trilocanam
Kala-Kalam-Ambujakasham-Akshashulam-Aksharam
Kashika-Pura-Adhinatha-Kalabhairavam-Bhaje. 2

Shula-Tanka-Pasha-Danda-Panim-Aadi-Karanam
Shyama-Kayam-Aadi-Devam-Aksharam-Nir-Aamayam
Bhima-Vikramam-Prabhum-Vichitra-Tandava-Priyam
Kashika-Pura-Adhinatha-Kalabhairavam-Bhaje. 3

Bhukti-Mukti-Dayakam-Prashasta-Caru-Vigraham
Bhakta-Vatsalam-Sthitam-Samasta-Loka-Vigraham
Nikvanan-Manojnya-Hema-Kinkini-Lasat-Katim
Kashika-Pura-Adhinatha-Kalabhairavam-Bhaje. 4

Dharma-Setu-Palakam-Tva-Adharma-Marga-Nashakam
Karma-Pasha-Mochakam-Su-Sharma-Dayakam-Vibhum
Svarna-Varna-Khesha-Pasha-Shobhitanga-Mandalam
Kashika-Pura-Adhinatha-Kalabhairavam-Bhaje. 5

Ratna-Paduka-Prabhabhi-Rama-Pada-Yugmakam
Nityam-Advitiyam-Istha-Daivatam-Niramjanam
Mrtyu-Darpa-Nashanam-Karala-Damshtra-Mokshanam
Kashika-Pura-Adhinatha-Kalabhairavam-Bhaje. 6

Atta-Hasa-Bhina-Padmaja-Anda-Kosha-Samtatim
Drshti-Pada-Nashta-Papa-Jalam-Ugra-Shasanam
Ashta-Siddhi-Dayakam-Kapala-Malika-Dharam
Kashika-Pura-Adhinatha-Kalabhairavam-Bhaje. 7

Bhuta-Sangha-Nayakam-Vishala-Kirti-Dayakam
Kashi-Vasa-Loka-Punya-Papa-Shodhakam-Vibhum
Niti-Marga-Kovidam-Puratanam-Jagatpatim
Kashika-Pura-Adhinatha-Kalabhairavam-Bhaje. 8

Kalabhairava-Ashtakam-Pathanti-Ye-Manoharam
Jnana-Mukti-Sadhanam-Vicitra-Punya-Vardhanam
Shoka-Moha-Dainya-Lobha-Kopa-Tapa-Nashanam
Prayanti-Kalabhairava-Angri-Sanidhim-Nara-Dhruvam. 9

About the Author

G. Varun Yadav is an engineering graduate by qualification and an acclaimed martial arts teacher by passion. He is a dedicated practitioner and instructor of Kalaripayattu, the ancient Indian combat system, and the author of the book Kalaripayattu: India's Own Combat Culture. In addition to Kalaripayattu, Varun is a practitioner of other combat systems, like Silambam, Kali and Muay Thai, showcasing his diverse exposure and experience in martial arts. Based in Mysuru, Karnataka, he runs his martial arts academy, Kalari Sadhana: Mysuru, where he is committed to preserving and propagating India's rich martial heritage, with a special emphasis on Kalaripayattu.An ardent follower of Sanatana Dharma, Varun integrates his spiritual practice into his life and teaching. He has been devoted to mantra meditation for several years, reflecting his holistic approach to physical and spiritual well-being.

You can connect with the author through:

* Email: varungokulyadav@gmail.com

* Instagram: @varungokulyadav | @KalariSadhana: Mysuru